THE
RED
BUDDHA

poems by
Maia Penfold

Some of these poems have appeared over the years in the following magazines, anthologies and books:

Bear
Beloit Poetry Journal
Canadian Forum
Citadel
Clinton Street
Connections
Denali
Ellensburg Anthology
Green's Magazine
Heavy Bear
Invisible City
Mother's Milk
Once More With Feeling
Other Side
Poetic Space
Room
Seizure Magazine
Specimen 73
Stonecloud
The Bridge
The Vagabond Anthology
Tidepools
Vagabond
Wormwood Review

Done with Mirrors, a collection of poems published by Vagabond Press in 1975.

Lost Generation, #6 in the Vagabond Press White Paper Series, published in 1983.

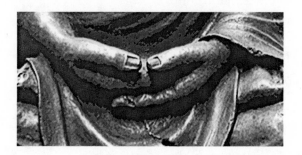

CONTENTS

continued...

CONTENTS ...*continued*

II.

III.

IV.

NEW WORLDS

As a kid in Canada I was a voracious reader. When I learned I could take an armful of books home from the Prince Albert Public Library, I started out with a huge heavy illustrated volume of stories from the Bible and puzzled and puzzled over *The Merchant and the Pearl of Great Price.* The guy gave all his money and worldly goods in exchange for one lone pearl. What happened next? How, I wondered, did he get along with no money for food, for shoes? It seemed to me it was not a practical decision and would lead to a lot of trouble on an everyday basis.

Later I learned poetry is like that, it demands everything you've got. And if you're really into it, it doesn't leave you much for necessities. The practice of poetry tends to arouse emotions of pity and contempt in our fellow creatures. And yet like that merchant who was so wise and so foolish we are driven to do it.

My favorite book was not the Bible or Lamb's *Tales from Shakespeare,* it was the *Ramayana,* the dancing world of the Hindu epic, shimmering with brilliant color, shining with light, a drumming world, of gods and kings and elephants, a world of happiness, of evil, of turmoil, triumph, and painful tragedy. My favorite god was Hanuman the monkey who opens his chest to reveal his living heart, who rescues the beautiful woman from the cruel king who captured her, Hanuman who makes a bridge of monkeys across the great water, little Hanuman who makes miracles.

Poetry is also like Hanuman, it demands our true heart, it demands we open our hearts to the world as it is, it makes

10 MAIA PENFOLD/The Red Buddha

its bridge of words taking us to places we never expected.

I fell in love with *Ramayana* because it is bigger, more colorful, more musical than the world of the Bible which to me was a very black and white angry vindictive world without joy. I preferred the world of the brothers Grimm with its love and respect for animals but that seemed a small village world with many stupid people. I loved the glorious world of the *Ramayana* embracing as it did all infinity, I love its reverence for the animals, the way it was a world of both/and, in which the universe is made of dualities and complexities, not a simple-minded sour world of one and only. I was happy to have found a more beautiful world.

And so I read shelf after shelf of books in the children's section and boldly approached the librarian who was a frightening person to me, announcing I had read everything in children's. "Now can I read adult books?" "You can read anything you want." Her ice-encrusted voice told me it was a matter of utter indifference to her whatever I read. And so I got into it all, plunging into pools of biography, splashing around in geology where time changed into new dimensions vast and infinite, I explored worlds of science with Lord Rutherford's marvelous *Chemical Discovery and Invention in the 20th Century.* Lord Byron showed me poetry could be made of ordinary casual talk, he was good at sarcastic edges, his words could slash like a scimitar. "There is a pleasure in the pathless woods, there is a rapture on the lonely shore...I love not man the less but nature more..."

I loved that library, books filled with ancient sorrows, with courage, with spirit. Made with the heart and mind and hand of man. I was quite drunk, totally intoxicated like Emily Dickinson, "I taste a liquor never brewed..."

And so eventually of course I had to one way or another try my own hand at it. I began as a reporter and a columnist writing reviews of art exhibitions. And then for years I devoted myself to painting until I got to a place where I could see I needed to make a huge leap into joining painting and sculpture. It was the next new place for me. And I just didn't see how I could do it and at that point I decided to get back into writing which I had left off many years before.

It would be, I thought, at least five years before I would be able to write anything anyone would value. To my immense surprise within a year I found myself doing readings at which strangers, total strangers rushed up to hug me! A group of musicians with drums and guitars had the idea to accompany me improvising loud rock music as I read "You Think He's Crazy." Periodicals in Toronto, Ontario and Madison, Wisconsin published my work. Bukowski accepted my poems for his *Laugh Literary and Man the Humping Guns*. "When I finish reading a poem," he wrote me, "I don't want to feel silk on my hands, I don't want to feel onionskin, I want to feel blood." I was invited to take part in readings with Bukowski, Paul Vangelisti, and John Thomas. More often than not I was the only woman on stage, the token woman. It was an odd feeling, a difficult feeling.

In 1974 I sent John Bennett of Vagabond Press a poem, "If You Read Hans Christian Andersen." He wrote back immediately telling me how on a high bank above the Yakima River where he'd gone to read his mail, the newspaper headlines were Richard Nixon, how he read my poem and Nixon was completely obliterated from his mind. Could I, he asked, send a book-length manuscript of poems?

And so *Done With Mirrors* was born, published with beautiful front and back silkscreen covers by the artist George Stillman who created a disarmingly simple and powerful image of transformation.

My alliance and friendship with Bennett continues to this day. As though he inhabits the vast panorama of the Mahabarata he does his pyrotechnic dance on the other side of the Cascades juggling and throwing knives, singing out words of fire, painting portraits of cowboys, lassoing the most beautiful women, walking his dog, describing the flight of birds and the inimitable gestures of five-year-old boys and still now that he's actually white-haired (!) giving us the great gift of wonder, the full range of emotion, illuminating worlds.

Probably the most requested poem at readings has been "Shit." The title seems to stun those who aren't familiar with the poem and often at readings someone in the audience calls out "Whaaat?" or "Pardon?" like they can't believe their ears. So I say "The title of this poem is 'Shit.'" Whatever expectations people may have at that point are not met, instead I take the audience on a wildly wonderful rollercoaster ride and before I've read the last line there's an eruption of the loudest most triumphantly spontaneous and unrestrained applause. Makes me feel like an alchemist transmuting dross into delight.

—*Maia Penfold*

A FEW WORDS FROM THE EDITOR

Maia Penfold, known at the time as Gerda Penfold, drifted into my life in 1974 via an envelope packed with poems. I read those poems in one setting, published them and others in a chapbook titled *Done with Mirrors*, and from that point on, over the next turbulent thirty-six years, Maia has been a spiritual and creative running mate who remains fiercely independent and disinclined to compromise.

She is a force of nature, no less so at the age of 82 than when she was a young girl in Saskatchewan and a young woman in Los Angeles and San Francisco, and her poetry is charged with this force, an elixir of wonder and innocence, biting wit and easy sophistication, an intelligence that drills to the core. She may be the most overlooked poet of the second half of the 20th century, and it came to me (as these things tend to do) in a flash of inspiration that I needed to collect as many of her poems as I could locate and put them into book form—Maia's life has been hard and nomadic, and many of her poems have been lost along the way. Not long after that I found myself on a ferry to Bainbridge Island off the coast of Washington where Maia then lived.

It was a magic couple of days. Maia has some health problems that keep her confined to bed or in a wheelchair, but I jump-started her old car and we tooled around the island, ate salmon in a fish house, drove along the ocean shore. We went through the poems with Maia lying regally in her bed stroking her cat Thomas Penfold and me next to the bed spinning around in the wheelchair, calling out for Chinese, the winter Olympics in the background on the TV with the volume down, taking turns reading the poems out loud, saying, "Yes, yes," or "No, no," shaping a book with deceptive ease like a couple of seasoned sorcerers.

Maia had it in her head to call the book *Grand Canyon*, but when I read the long poem "Across the Street" we laughed so hard we had tears in our eyes and our jaws and the backs of our head ached while Thomas Penfold looked from one to the other with mild disapproval and Maia said, picking up on an image in the poem: "Let's call the book *The Red Buddha*." That, young poets, is how it's done in the real world.

And here it is in your hands, *The Red Buddha*, a book that is as close as it gets to the collected poems of Maia Penfold, a woman who has burned her way through life with passion, joy and awe.

—John Bennett
May 21, 2010

Maia Penfold & John Bennett, Ellensburg, Washington, 1981

The Red Buddha

I

WORDS BECOME MAGIC AGAIN

pick themselves up and dust off
the time that held them
words walk again
listening precisely to the sounds
that slide through the thin
sweet air

choice they say

harlot they laugh conjuring old-fashioned
colors deep as stained glass
the light streaming through

thief ancient one
the words are solemn

comrade they say poking each
other in the ribs like schoolboys

they walk through the double doors
of the old text to the wild king
who saw
the handwriting on the wall

i see the graffiti
of manhattan as wondrous art
illuminations
of the heart despised insisting
on love insisting

i see the long light of morning

now that
the words are here again
singular and savage

trying on their
new shoes

ACROSS THE STREET

in that rough brooklyn neighborhood
the commotion

i leaned out my fourth floor window
nine in the morning
they were going to work
a small circle
stopped
looking up
12 red brick stories
tension in the air

first i thought
a suicide
then he
leaned out
the second floor window
a shifting circular knot of people
someone would move on
another move in

he addressed them
addressed everyone
within range of his voice
addressed people walking
by addressed people leaning out
windows

clean up your lives!
what have you got?
you've got nothing!
you've got shit!
that's all you've got!

i'm getting rid of all this shit
he yelled and kitchen
pots and pans and
plates went flying out
the window crashing
on the sidewalk below

he held out an armful of record albums
this is shit! he said
i don't want it!

I DON'T WANT IT! and records
went flying down to the sidewalk

why don't you clean up your life? he
harangued and hurled out
the television threw
out the toilet paper
sweeping like a white
banner to the ground

they were trying to snatch
up the records
watching out so
they wouldn't be hit

by something else
coming down

he held out a handful of money
green bills and asked
d'you know what this is?
they all stretched out their arms
ready for the catch
it's shit! he said
and
the green bills floated down

the green plants in
their pots dirt and all
went out
he was holding
a small doll her skirt
yellow satin ruffles
for the first time reluctant
hesitating
selecting one woman
to receive the doll
very carefully
gently
let her go
to be caught by those
outreaching arms

he was gone awhile

when he appeared again
he had a mattress in his arms
tried to force it out the window

tried with all his
muscular force to heave it out
and the crowd laughed
but the mattress wouldn't go through

he threw out chairs
tables lamps
smashed up piled up
on the sidewalk people
snatching grabbing dodging
it was a crazy party

he threw out books photo albums

you're crazy! somebody yelled

he was still pitching stuff out

that's where you're wrong he said
you think this is something?
this is shit
i don't want shit in my life
i want my life to be clean

they didn't know what he meant
he threw out the clorox and the tide
he threw
out the rugs he
threw out everything

and gradually he seemed
to start feeling better
like it really was

making him feel
better to get rid of
it all
but he couldn't get
that mattress out

just as the police car pulled up
he put the big red buddha
on the windowsill
to occupy the place
where he had been

they get him handcuffed
push him into the car

i want a happy ending
for the handcuffed man

but only
the big red buddha remains

mass produced replica
of the real thing

DIANE NYAD SWIMS A CIRCLE

around manhattan island
breasting the muck the
bilge filled hudson and the
east river thick with effluvia

around the magical city
gleaming financial towers
the empire state and the
chrysler building always for
me with its great gorilla
king kong invisibly embracing it
more real than real life
more real than the corporate
ladders real men clamber up
manufacturers hanover trust
chase manhattan chemical bank

(and the obelisk in central park
my plane coming in to kennedy
circled over

and over the waves
that lapped long island and
the white tiny sails of boats
no bigger than my fingernail)

diane nyad swims
around manhattan wearing

goggles and a white bathing cap
pulling herself through it
on her own shoulders her
own arms and legs kicking
splashing churning on refusing
to sink or quit going on
going on

(new york always reminding me
irrationally of king nebuchadnezzar
on hands and knees
chewing grass
nebuchadnezzar with
everything coins can buy
mad as the mist and snow
on his knees in central park)

while diane nyad swims
around the island stroke
after stroke and king kong
embraces the spire of the
chrysler building
roaring snatching small
planes out of the air

i don't know how
diane did it
and i'm not sure why

when there are worlds
west of the hudson

HE DOESN'T LAUGH

he doesn't laugh
not once
in the whole bible
that's it   that's what
i want   that's what
i'm waiting for
to hear god laugh

the great sudden gust
of wind
flung open the french windows
letting in sun & wind
i walked over
i closed them as
a pale old man
in a rocking chair
two backyards away
looked up

IN THE DREAM
I LIVED

near the foundry
maybe half a dozen people
sitting around sprawled in chairs
with tall clear glasses
bright ice chunks in them

we discussed the use of ice
in the process of steel making

from where we sat
we could see the orange roar
of the flames in the furnaces
could see the molten metal
glow like lava

hear it all crackle and hiss
as we
sip cool liquid
in tall clear glasses
casually
carrying on our conversation

THE FOLIAGE
BEGINS TO
RATTLE

scissors fall apart
the woman stands outside
afternoons she's there
mornings early evenings

in a pale blue bathrobe
a longer paler blue nightgown
under it
scuffy slippers on the feet

she looks at the sky
feeds the crumbs to the descending
pigeons and looks at the
passersby with a face as flat
as a newspaper

shuffling among the plants and pigeons
she has a secret pact with the sky
and has no need to ever dress
any way but the way she does

i see a halo like neon
in the shape of a coffin
around her whole body

HE WOULD MAKE A FINE BANK ROBBER

His face is so forgettable
Not that his features are unattractive
But that he could be anything
An aerospace engineer
An insurance company executive
A checkout cashier
Even so as the bank teller
Said to him questioning
His signature, "This isn't
The signature we have on file"
And how he signed again
And somehow it still
Wasn't what they had
In the files
And then to prove his identity
He took out identity cards
With his photo
And it wasn't his face
It was the bearded face
Of another man not his
Clean shaven responsible
Honest straightforward
No nonsense face
It was another face

And the more he tried
To demonstrate who he really
Was the more his identity
Faded and flickered and blurred
He was no stranger to that teller
There had been transactions
Between them over a period of 18 months
But she didn't know
Whose face it was
Whose photo it was
Before her eyes the photo
Turns to fire spontaneous
Combustion the brown edges
Convulse wither into flame
Writhe and smoke
For a moment his burning
Face floats and freezes
In grey ash a ghost
He could be anyone
Anything anywhere

That teller wants him to be
One person or nobody
She doesn't want to see
His hair turn to blue fire
She doesn't want him messing
With the mirrors she lives by

THE MAD SCIENTIST

Is a well known
Figure in our fiction
And movies of the last 20 years
In which anything can be done by
Pushing a button hardly larger
Than an aspirin or an anacin tablet
In spite of all the apparatus
The scientist never wins in the stories
In the distance coming closer
I hear his recorded laughter
It gives me a nice shaky feeling
It sounds so real

THE CRAZY HOUSES ARE FULL

of Christs
who really mean it but
haven't made it

It came to the guy from Galilee
in the desert or someplace
that he
needed help

but the Christs in Camarillo
and maybe even Atascadero
try
to do it
alone

THE CHILD ARTIST

always starts with the heart

she draws the purple
outline and fills it with
scarlet and it
becomes a scarf
an ascot heart under
a smiling chin
the high heeled small
shoes far below it

4 yrs old she draws
a pink heart and out
spread arms above it
a robe
hangs
down straight from
the wrists a robe you
can see through to
the heart and
other organs a floating
liver a kidney
a stomach a
wild wiggle of guts

she makes infinite
variations on her heart
theme which is so clearly
inexhaustible

here it is a décolleté
heart torso tight above
the wide tutu of the
ballerina

and there the heart
is held out big and
bold in the hand
without hesitation
or reservation
that one has a big body
a football pennant
in one hand and an axe
in the other
his heart has slipped
down to the lower
parts of his body and
appears to be dripping
thick drops of
dark blood

and this woman is
from the 18th century
of cinderella
and marie antoinette
she has many fingers
more even than ten
her heart is down
around her waist
which does not detract
from the
extravaganza of her outfit

the artist knows
her A, B, C's and
proves it
when she gets up to P, U, she
turns up
the volume of her voice and
laughs she can't help
it
P, U, she says

then she demonstrates
her pirouette
she is so good
she couldn't be
any better

but her momma says stop that
right now i mean it
there are people living
under us

stop that dancing
right now

looking down at her
offending feet

she stops

THE LIGHT IS AFRICAN

an audience appears
i take them through
i speak in german

this man he has a knife
(we look at the knife)
heavy plastic
resembling a kitchen grater
a strange knife

the small audience gasps
ahhhhhhhh

i show them the other compartment
contains
shoe polish a brush and a rag
the man also owns this i say
the audience nods understanding that this
is evidence of a role in
life the audience nods
for some time

the other man i tell them
has nothing

the audience stares at me
we are in africa but that doesn't matter

there is hot sand under our feet
but that is irrelevant

i tell them the man with the
knife and the shoe polish is
a doctor (in my opinion this is
not important but i let the audience
decide for themselves) the man with
nothing is a prisoner

which man i ask
will live longer?

(i prefer to avoid false melodrama
i do not say which man will live?)

we look out across
the sands
in the distance
we see two men
approaching

WHERE A WOMAN KEEPS HOUSE

the air crisply clear
milk in milk white jugs
poured by a woman painted
by vermeer a woman solid
and strong keeps a good
house

an
opulent bouquet tulips streaked
orange and red flamboyant
roses wide open and with fallen
petals a soft explosion a lavishness
the stems are not straight
change direction like a woman
who has loosened her beautiful
clothes half undressed
her soft fullness
her dress slipping down

laundry snapping on the line
bellying in and out

YOUR HANDS
HAVE LEFT

a print on my face that does not erase
you have changed the climate i live in

it is true i will never be the same again

the furniture was rearrangeable

it's just that the time you left
for the last time as you closed the door
without looking back
the walls fell down and the roof

since then i've lived with the leaves
the wind
like a bird without wings

my table and chairs there
out on the lawn

the walls are down for good

THERE IS SOMETHING HE DOESN'T HAVE

some part missing which he
refuses or is unable to identify
in fact his almost total concern
is to keep us from that knowledge
it keeps him in constant
motion like someone in a cold
room lying on a bed
with one blanket and that
blanket too short so now
the feet are out now the
shoulders and always some
-thing is shivering

NO LONGER HIS WIFE

she's married a man
who is she tells her relatives in vermont
as totally different from jim as you
can possibly imagine this man
raises horses that graze in the pasture
beside their breakfast windows
in the silver mists of early dawn

this man is dependable this man
does all the housework and
gripes about it she says the house
which is registered as historical
is his passion it is like
a museum to him and he is
the curator i am impressed by
how the great stairway glows
how windows gleam

it is so spotless and beautiful
i hardly dare walk or breathe
in it upstairs they put me
in a bedroom with a fine film
of dust over it and when i
lie down the mattress crashes to
the floor i go down to tell
them about it that always

happens he says and with a sigh
goes up to set it right

in the morning he drives me
to my conference i compliment
him on the beauty of the house

it's a lot of work he says
his jaws tight his lips pressing
out the words ironing anger in
his tone tells me he is
insufficiently appreciated
and taken advantage of he teaches
french for a living

i remember wet towels
on the bathroom floor in that
other house with that other man
plants needed water dogs
yelped and barked
the exuberance of it

everything needed something
and said so
everything was only pretending
to be tame had been
wild yesterday and would be
wild again tomorrow
that yellow light in willy's
eyes that sheen on the

dog's fur that primitive posturing
of the rooster and the hens
the parade of tulips
the leaves held secrets
flowers opened their wide corollas
everything teetering in
shafts of sunlight on a cliff's edge

i miss that the wide open
hospitality steaks
we cooked at sunset
eaten under a sky
sprinkled with stars

i miss that

stepping carefully out of his car

i miss that

KAFKA
WATCHES ME

i have no
cockroaches in my
kitchen
but kafka stares at me
over the sink his face
on the white wall
and to my left beside
the refrigerator i see sunshine
as a strange substance
and through glass

i have painted my refrigerator
orange

LOOKING
OUT

at the pacific
fat lazy orange cat
your meow is almost inaudible

today i feel like that
too fat too lazy
to move muscles of mind
into poems

slow everything slow
today some other jonah sits
in the dark whale belly

i yawn

and do my nails

ARMS OF
THE GIANT
MANDALA

open up
here meditating
my window the postcard blue
sky of san francisco and high buildings
hit by the sun
checkered by their own shadows
two aborigines leap up
into air
with their
long long spears
poised forever
in photograph
taken in toronto
where
they leaped into that light
forever and dancing in
it and frozen forever
in photograph like
a hieroglyph of time
in which we
are all included
ping! of the present
the clock crucified

I'M AN INDIAN
HE EXPLAINED

he flew down the aisle
on the mission street bus
spreading his waving arms
a flying eagle
sitting down beside me
telling me quietly
this is all mine
i own all this
his arms pointing to the grand canyon
the mississippi the oregon mountains
waving his arms laughing
i'm an indian he explained

telling me about the last time
he was in jail

steel bus bars around us

everybody staring at us

what kind of an indian
are you? he asks me
and i tell him
i'm a blond apache
he doesn't
laugh

stroking his cheekbones
you have the bones
he nods
you have the bones

we get off the bus now
he's waiting for the kearny
and invites me to accompany him
but i'm waiting for the stockton

looking down at his reflection
you see me standing here he says
an indian drunk like a fool

i see the rain what can we say
when rain's
erased the stars?

SAN FRANCISCO
LIFESTYLE

he was one of the folk figures
(hero would not be the right word)
of market street

a scrawny unkempt thin bird
of a man
he would rush into a phone booth
and check the coin return
then he'd crouch down in there
becoming invisible
and after the right interval
and careful calculations on his part
he'd rush out speeding to
the next phone booth check the
coin return crouch down wait
for just the right time and trying
to go so fast he'd be nearly
invisible
hit the next one check for
coins and crouch down

it was a difficult and lonely
lifestyle he'd adopted living
from payphone to payphone

and never completely
becoming invisible as he
rushed from one to the next
his coat his pants his hair
his shoes flapping

it was one of many marginal
lifestyles on market street
but it did have a certain dash
and style of its own a kind
of integrity to it

sometimes i wonder what
happened
to his kryptonite
and what will happen
when he
finds it again
in the phone booth

giving him the power
to fly over taco stands
and the ability
to make us look up to him

OH THERE
THAT

wound in your back
healed into an indentation
big enough for me to put
my thumbprint in
touching you there
where you were broken
and healed over whole
again

you won't tell what
happened stabbed in the back
or struck by shrapnel in
vietnam you will only say
it hurts

we walk into a restaurant and
you go for the corners
your back to the wall
and make me sit
facing it (and you)

you ask for massage and
harder pressures you wince
and something twists
but no, it won't do

i take you to dr. hans wong
on sacramento in
chinatown
and where it says
occupation on the
application you ask me
what shall i put?

and i say put mover
that covers a lot
and it connects with
what you're here for
you smile writing down

and the standing buddha
framed on the wall
a modest watercolor
he has his feet firmly
on the clouds
and smiles serenely
at the sky

dr. wong takes you in
and later you tell me
how
he didn't use x-rays
just ran his hands
down your bare back
on both sides of your

spine and pressed there
something snapped
the pain never came back

and he did it in 3 seconds
with his bare hands

but you still go for
the corners your back
to the wall taking
no chances

I WALK IN THE FINANCIAL DISTRICT

of san francisco
wearing live snakes dancing
over my whole body

the secretaries look away
the bank teller does not say hello
he does not like the way
i withdraw dollars so easily
and deposit money so often
he looks at me suspiciously

my live snakes dance over my whole body

i walk down montgomery street
and see my old boss who
is six feet six
his eyebrows are extraordinary
my old aquarius boss

we look at each other eye to eye
his eyes do not flinch
his white hair recognizes me
my friendly laughter
says hello again

my snakes dance remembering
when i typed his letters

when i scribbled shorthand from his speech
when i answered his phone
when i greeted his clients and visitors

remembering how i slid through
his doors like a secretary

my old boss who did crossword puzzles
behind closed doors
while randy hearst tried
to reach him
i remember randy hearst's voice
wanting to talk to my old boss

about a daughter behind bars
a daughter who made the cover
of time magazine
with a machine gun in her hands
i remember the voice of katherine hearst
waiting to be connected

i walk down montgomery street
live snakes dancing
over my whole body walking
in shoes

WE JOINED ALICE

through the looking-glass
found ourselves and each other
in such transparent joy
we had to celebrate and sing
we had to dance and get naked

we had to listen to jimi hendrix
do the star spangled banner as a savage anthem
of no mercy
on vietnam bombs bursting in air we had to
recognize each other and we had to say it
make love not war and mean it

kesey took us on a wild ride
through america into the pain of it
into the belly of the beast of it
into the black & white south & north of it
sinful arrogance hideous cruelty of it

kesey took us into
the funny farms of america where
nurse ratched ruled the roost

he took us to the western edges of our continent
to the vastness of the pacific the whole of it
parked his bus there

at the edge
of everything it said further

its destination spelled out up there above
the driver's seat
FURTHER

i couldn't help applauding
what're you doing? my daughter-in-law asked

what does it look like i'm doing?
i'm applauding

what are you applauding? she asked

i'm applauding the bus i told her

under the blinding california sky
beyond golden gate park
i was applauding

why? glenda persisted

because i love it
i love this bus

here it is
ahead of it nothing
but thousands and thousands of miles of water
and it says further

i love it

i couldn't stop i just couldn't stop
applauding the lovely outrageous unstoppable
effrontery of it just then ken

kesey although i didn't know it
was ken kesey until much much later
waved me toward the bus
he gestured up into the bus

d'you wanna get on the bus?
he asked with that smile of invitation

can i just look inside?

no
you're either on the bus
or you're off the bus

and that was that

that bus
is still part of my heart

parked pointing to hawaii
pointing to the undulating grass
skirts the plinking ukulele music
the hot sand pointing to the kimonos of japan
the aborigines of australia the temples of india
fueled by desire
for life more spacious
more loving life less hurtful life
there waiting
for all of us for each of us
if we only have sense enough
to get on the bus
and get with it

The Red Buddha

Maia Penfold with one of her paintings, 1972

WE VALUE HIM

Not only for
The paintings on their canvases
But also for that ear
He cut off
And the fact that
He didn't listen

PAUL KLEE

the paintings of paul klee
speaking so many languages
so fluidly
traveling under sea wandering to morocco
picturing domes of mosques
a gentle world of windows and doors
a veiled woman among so many silences
a multiplicity of eyes
the panther black on black
on the high wire birds twittering
the actor's mask trembling with
possibility after possibility
a faraway music approaches

time unfolding its many years

while angels write small letters
to the future

where we are now

ascending
the ornate stairway

CRAZY
CLYFFORD STILL

unriddled the rocks
his paintings like thunder eggs
and onyx like fire and flame
solidified caught held
immobile and alive
a wall of red fire with dark veins
and clusters centered with white
brighter than diamonds more rare
more white more light the
inferno still alive in the heart of it
the heart pulse there and
the raw desolation the cry
the sheer air terror
taken by the throat
he would get on his knees
for no man
you get on your knees to them
he said and you'll walk on your knees
for the rest of your life
he lived in a cheap place
with linoleum on the floor

GEORGIA
O'KEEFE

bones white architecture
verisimilitude of light
these skin thin canvases
provide more than beauty

it is the extraordinary at the heart
of the ordinary

conflagration of canna lily
petals of white sweet peas

with the soft knife edge of her lines
she demolishes the limits
of our sight
and
like a midwife she introduces
us to the sky

true artists are dangerously
generous

OLDENBURG
FEELS

like a manicurist filing
the wooden keys of his
soft typewriter
i feel like part
of a christmas card
in my vw driving through
the cascade mountains
my headlights picking out

the white banks the fat white
crystals down through
the clear air

the next morning i wake up
in a motel
on a high riverbank where the
year before
the spring floods had bitten out
huge chunks of earth
including houses
falling roof over floor
floor over roof

i stand on
an edge of air

ARSHILE GORKY
WAS HE
THE ONE

who hung himself in a barn
with a necktie? or was it
mark rothko?
or was it both of
them? i know franz kline
ran into a tree on long
island after the collector
in the village bar said to
him he would pay
ten thousand a case
of jack daniels and
a triumph sports car
for that painting

he explained kline
would drink the whiskey
drive the car and kill himself

the painting would be
worth sixty thousand the
day after the obituary and
he the collector would
have netted a profit of
thirty thousand after
having deducted the cost
of the car and the whiskey

that painting of gorky's hangs
in my mind and a small
print of it from newsweek is
scotchtaped to my bathroom wall
it is made up of twinned lobes
testicles buttocks and breasts
a red plow runs through
it on a field which is not
the color of sky or the color
of wheat

the artists hand us messages
from a zone of war messages
that look like the entrails of pike
and the parts of an aircraft
assembly line

but we
have been inoculated
with a virus
that makes us
turn their messages
into nothing

but money

LA PESADILLA

that enraged and frightened woman of goya
i can feel the perspiration of fear under
her forty year old armpits i can taste
the sour saliva from the tongue of the bull on which
she is riding feel his wet nostrils hear her
shrill screaming
and what is there to do about it?

    her naked thighs where her dress has come apart
    are not attractive
    nor the teeth in her wide mouth
    she is not the least attractive

the mindless bull plunging her forward
does not care where he is taking her

    once when she was young
    she was beautiful
    and he came to her
    disguised as a prince with the
    rose colored gifts of promises
    once when she was young
    they made long journeys together
    through imaginary countries
    that now have come to this

she cannot stop him
and she does not want to
and she can think of
nothing else to do

HE STRIPPED
ALL THAT
AWAY

the obsessions that possessed him
as he became famous and more famous
capturing on canvas the precise
transparency sheer over a
shoulder
the soft velvet cascade
over the round swell
of the breast the delicate oval
of the face the stance
firm footed the proud posture
the hair a tumble of curls
the quality of the eyes
all so lovely so real
so alive they applauded
and applauded

their money flowed
into his hands

then he stripped away all that
tore off the treasures
peeled it all off
to below the precious
appearances
he stripped away
the prettiness

the frills the little medals
the delicate parasols
the ornate buckles on the shoes
the poised fan flickering
the sweet surface charms
slammed the door
on all the drawing rooms
and went to where
that place where the blood is
the killing floor
where the helpless humans
throw their arms up
open mouthed riddled
with bullets where the bull
lies in the blood while
el matador bows in his
exquisite costume to the
roaring crowd

in his last and later years
Goya painted human bats
flapping like phantoms
through a thick air of
ignorance he painted monsters
with a taste for flesh
he painted greed
he painted raving appetites
he painted coils of ambition
he painted maggots
crawling

on the faces of the powerful

AMONG
THE ROCKS
AND THE
FLOWERS

of course i know what i'm doing
georgia o'keefe said what kind
of an idiot do they take me for?

painting fertility equipment of flowers
pink cup blossom hibiscus
morning glory corollas invite bees to buzz by
orchids openly offer themselves
hummingbirds drink from down dangling fuchsia
orange poppies do their level best
peonies scent the heavy happy air

her last canvases fill the gallery
to the horizon with an infinity
of clouds seen from above resplendent sunlit

astounded by o'keefe's vision
the sensational simplicity the elegance
the size of it o'keefe has me up there

like 5 year old rowan flying
seattle to portland talking
on the phone to his mom he tells her
mom we flew up through the clouds

we flew
over the clouds
right up where god is!

she paints the bones white austerity
she paints the landscape breathing holiness
enclosing unfolding the mystery

she paints our own true history
among the rocks and flowers
and flying

MY PHOTOGRAPHS

The photographs on my walls are all snow scenes
And the escape tunnel from the launching site
At Cape Kennedy which is somehow still
Cape Canaveral in my mind
It rhymes in my mind with caravan carnival
And vernal and infernal and there is something
Of an illusion cast upon a veil about it all
Like a black and white film with a contemporary
Soundtrack cast on a wide white screen
There is a scream about it
And that tunnel photograph is like
 an open mouth of horror
Opened so wide like that famous scream on the bridge
By the Norwegian woodcut artist Edvard Munch
Holding its ears to its head with its hands
And way at the back of that open throat the little
White man walking dangles like a tonsil

SHIT

i've seen so many art exhibitions
in canada wrote a weekly news-
paper column, reviews of art ex-
hibitions and interviews with
artists now
i have an idea for an exhibition
at the l.a. county art museum
shit from the
asshole of each artist with
the time and date appended
and maybe in the catalog
his menu for the day before
and as added insight
each artist to have the right
to display his shit as he sees
fit like edward keinholz
could give us nice warm
fresh shit simply
placed on a copy of the
l.a. times
larry bell could show his shit
inside the clean simple
design of a glass box held together
with chrome strips the glass
specially treated so that
it is iridescent
kenneth price's dried shit
spray painted
short cylinders in
primary colors

the possibilities are endless
imagine your own shit show
and imagine it elegantly
installed
at the l.a. county
museum and on the night
of the opening imagine
one of the gorillas from
the san diego zoo one of
the most famous shit
throwers in california
(when i was there
an audience was standing
around waiting in tense
anticipation and a little
lady with glasses and one of
those dresses fifty year old
ladies wear said
to the guard when does
he do it? and the guard
said he could do it
anytime and i walked
further on and then i heard
a scream behind me
and i knew he'd done it)
i think it would be
a sensational show

The Red Buddha

III

STURM AND DRANG

the words are heavy indigo
shot with lightning shudders
advancing relentless
a downpour we are wet soaked
to the skin with rain
sturm and drang
the words wring us
out this is my mother tongue
these words blumen and baum
and himmel these huge words
were my first words large
useless as beached whales
become equally offensive
when transported to canada
all my words were worthless

they spoke other words
under the smaller sky
their words weighed less
they were light as dresses
some words like shoe
stayed the same while
kuh became cow
die katze became the cat
transformations like clouds
were in the air some words
like cowboys puzzled me and there

were buckaroos too in the movies
i heard the song go to sleep
my little buckaroo
there were windows and doors
lumber and ink
and wink my angst was immense

so was my appetite
for books full of words
and oh the wide wonder of the world
that could be described in so many
ways

midorsin migeesegau the
cree woman said saying it's
a nice day her syllables soft
floating like feathers her words
a song of praise

OUR TRAIN

We crossed the railroad
Tracks every day
Ran down
The diagonal path
Through the vegetable patches
To see
Who could be
The first to get there
Before that black train
Trembling the track
And loud in our ears
On the steel
Rails and sometimes
One
Of us
Crawled under the 9th Avenue
Culvert and the train
Ran right over us
Trembling us and so loud
Nobody heard us
As we cried loud
As we could
Screaming at the top
Of our children's voices
With crazy wild joy
At twelve o'clock
As that train our train
Went by

YOU GO
BACK TO IT

to your earliest
childhood to where
your brother fell through
the hole in the outhouse
and vera lifted the lid
at the back
so he could crawl
out

lucky just lucky
we were playing
ante eye over
over the roof of the shed
when it happened

mom screaming and screaming
dipping him in the barrel
of rainwater
us kids we couldn't stop
laughing even though he
was still crying

now that he's a professor
at the university of saskatchewan
and an internationally recognized

authority on underwater
surveying for minerals

i wonder if george remembers
that summer when
he was 4 years old

when he fell into
some deep shit

and survived

MY SISTER IN IDAHO

in her brand new mega house
with the best the latest of everything
opens the oven door
and pulls out the oldtime roasting pan
two chickens done to perfection
the air we breathe fills with fragrance

but it's the pan itself that gets me
it goes back to the 30's
I can't believe i'm seeing it again it
brings such a huge
chunk of childhood with it

big bulging oval enamelware cream color
with green trim

it transports me back
to how our dad in the depths
of the depression got meat going out
in the snowy woods snaring rabbits

I remember three rabbits right in there
stretched out brown and delicious
mom and dad laughed because
my favorite part was the neck

how my father gave german lessons
for twenty-five cents an hour

one day given a nickel
instead of the the quarter he'd earned
he walked back a mile back across the frozen river
to get the coin he deserved

that green and cream roasting pan
brings it all back
look feel and smell of it

how somehow we always
had a fine meal on sunday
even if it was slim pickings
the rest of the week

sunday was always a celebration

we were celebrating our very
survival letting ourselves know
life was good we could laugh

surprised at the way happiness
came out of hiding
into full view that one day a week
and then jumped out of sight

my sister puts platters and bowls of food
on the tablecloth under the crystal chandelier

but i'm back in saskatchewan
on our day of triumph
over the bleakness
of the rest of the week

GONE WITH THE WIND

how it caught my schoolgirl mind
the crinolines moving like clouds
over the impossibly green and
impossibly wide lawns a world
of such whiteness such delicate
and exquisite elegance

so far from saskatchewan
i was as dazzled by it
as if it were tahiti

it was so far from me
that
swirling arrogance and those
smiling slaves but when
atlanta caught fire and the
town went down

my mind reeled back
to my neighbor's house on fire
manny and lorraine who walked
to school with me and their
dog dead against the locked door
trying to get out

the next day i walked through
what was left the roof was
gone the walls were black

and metal had melted even
the bodies were gone

standing inside looking up
i saw nothing but
december sky

when the city blazed
on the screen i saw manny
and lorrainne and their good dog
the way they were
the day before they died

snow covered the white
december ground and we
were dressed like eskimos
he held my
ink bottle in his
mitten while i
reached
into my
pocket for something

we were all
laughing and warm

in the cold fist
of this winter world

MY CHILDHOOD IN SASKATCHEWAN

included niagra falls on the
breakfast table the box of
nabisco shredded wheat on which
the water cascaded endlessly
falling cascade
the focus of my morning
meditation

in my
books of knowledge
20 volume encyclopedia there was
the great blondini walking across
the falls
blindfolded

and pushing a woman
in a wheelbarrow

who was not blindfolded
who could see

everything

while he walked putting
one blind foot in front of the
other

i was unable
to comprehend

her courage

unable
to comprehend

why she would trust
a blindman

with her life

why would she?

i kept asking myself
those schoolday mornings
in saskatchewan with

niagra falls thousands
of miles away

IN BELL'S DRUGSTORE

i was reading baudelaire
sitting in bell's drugstore in canada
surrounded by vapors turbulences
lumiére of baudelaire
like missouri caves
of huck finn and tom sawyer and
a voice startled me
said beside me

you should not read baudelaire

i looked into the face
of the man on the stool beside me
from ottawa teaching french
for the summer he said

a young girl like you
and his eyes and gestures elaborated
on my youngness and i asked him
quite seriously

what should i read?

and he said musset
alfred de musset

some days later he was walking on the campus
and i was going in the other direction

he said hello and i said
i'm reading musset

and he said

don't read too much of him

THEY WERE POOR BUT CLEAN

that was how
stories in the book of my
childhood would begin

in a town called prince albert
saskatchewan

they were poor but clean
and then

there was blood everywhere
in their house after the father
axed the children and the wife
he couldn't feed because he lost
his job and couldn't get a new
one he killed them with
his axe and then shot himself
with a gun and when it happened
a block from where i lived

i stood with everyone else
in front of that house
where it happened
the blood they said was
everywhere

that poor man! i heard them say
he didn't know he just didn't know
know what to do he lost
his mind!

i was six years old and

i was frozen to the ground
in hot summer and i
knew
grownups don't always know
what to do

everybody standing there
was scared
the kids the
fathers the
mothers
looking back on that
depression decade
what infuriates and makes
tears jump from my eyes
are those lines

they were poor but clean

in that depression decade when
even soap was scarce
no one of us
lived through
that day without being hurt
although buried deep as they

are we may have no scars
to show for it

may have forgotten
how we lived
poor
and filthy with fear

nobody wants
to remember how bad
it was

and how little it mattered
if we were clean if we
were good if we worked
hard
how little it mattered

how little
we mattered

in the winds of economic
war and folly
that caught us up and
smashed us up against the

walls of the small houses
in which we tried to live

our lives

THE HOUSE
OF GUISE

looking all the way back
in the rear view mirror
to the 14 year old girl in saskatchewan
where i was well aware
that like the rest of north america
i was in indian country

although already the cree people
were pushed and squeezed
into small reservations

but there was mrs guise next door
full blooded and beautiful married to
a marine engineer from scotland
now responsible for the functioning
of brewery equipment he knew about
steam pressure and mechanics
and the way he could play the fiddle
fast and faster

mrs guise listened to me
the way my mother didn't
her girls helen and eleanor guise
were my friends but it was the mom
i liked best
the way she gave me her full attention
as though i had things to say

worth listening to
i savored that
so delicious it was even better
than her blueberry pie

her husband's family tree she told me
included french nobility going back to
the duc de guise at the time
of mary queen of scots

i have no trouble believing
the banners of history unfurl such
improbabilities of lineage
such lines of blood
and bloodshed intertwined

later he son ernest gilbert guise
becomes the object of an immense
rcmp manhunt
for weeks ernie evades capture
but those hunters live up to their motto
they get their man

in vancouver her daughter helen
with her thick dark hair and the curves
of her body becomes a rosemary reid
swimsuit model

her daughter eleanor married to a
missionary
spends years in china

today i remember the house of guise
on the corner of 18th street and 9th avenue
there in prince albert saskatchewan
the year is 1942
history flows back to a queen beheaded
history goes forward to a son doomed to death

the two daughters
one a model the other in china
an emissary of the man from nazareth

today i remember
the house of guise
mother father son
those two young girls and

all our improbable lives

MRS HARRISON AND THE CANADIAN COPS

mrs harrison i never liked you
maybe it was because
you seemed the epitome of ignorance
short overflowing with fat
your face somehow squat and neckless
you waddled by our house
your rake and a hoe
over one shoulder on the way
to your vegetable garden
fat purple poppies
scattered all over big
nodding blossoms later
curious cute seed pods
us kids used to go in and snatch

we all said they were
opium
mrs harrison is growing
opium
finally
one day

two local cops came to call
on mrs harrison while she
was weeding

they talked to her about
regulations asked her
questions wanted her to sign
things

mrs harrison heaved
a big sigh
turned round delicately lifted
her cotton print dress
and with it there bare

"you can kiss my ass" she said

the two cops terrified
ran off up the hill

and never came back

TRAVELLED UP

to totem pole country
up to the shadow
of mt. arrowsmith

georgia strait
washes up driftwood debris
handfuls of sand dollars

round skeletons incised
with the five pointed star
a natural pentacle

grey roots branches
broken shells wet glitter

dawn is this bridge of light
from mainland mountains
to my feet

sun climbing
the ladder
of clouds

HERE ON THE SNOWDRIFTED MALHAT

road my brother and i
eight years ago brought my
father's ashes home

i held that grey cardboard box
that was so heavy and so small
in my lap in my two hands

and now on this road again

tears and images
of my father

my father in his boat in the fog
in englishman's bay and the
whales diving and leaping
around him poised him between
fear and joy
their great size and the great
joy and ease of their motion

my father alone with them
on the ocean unable to see
the shore

WHAT CULTURE
DO I HAVE?

the myths of the Greeks? of the Romans?
that stuff? that is my culture?
the teachers fed me like cottage cheese?
What did Zeus and Mercury have to do
with me?
the cranky lineage of British royalty
we had a lot of that in Canada
what did that have to do with me?
my 12 inch ruler with the names
and dates of all the British
monarchs printed like a ladder
on the back and on the front
of my exercise book little
Princess Margaret little Princess
Elizabeth in party dresses
what did it have to do
with me?
what culture do I have conjugating
Latin verbs recognizing the gender
of French nouns declining
German adjectives?

I'll take a handful of silverleaves
growing in the wind beside
the water and paste
a silver wreath
around the moon
in the darkness

they told me how far away the moon is in miles
if I stretch high enough I thought
I can touch it
with my fingertips
the way the way
the chokecherry branches touch it
they told me I couldn't
what can they say
now that I've swallowed it
and it
glows there
between my breasts
looking back up at the sky?

HAVING REACHED THREE SCORE AND TEN

it leaps out
that afternoon
in saskatchewan in the brilliant sun
pedaling my bicycle over the crunch
of gravel road
the world was all around me
and i was in it i was entirely in it
and then a car approached slowing down
a man and a woman their arms out the windows
waving wildly they yelled the war is over
the war is over
they never stopped
i was stunned
to hear it

lying in the grass a book of poetry
and dry sweet summer smell of hay
squinting up into the sky tiger moths
flying through the luminous clouds
that must feel so fine so free
but those were the tiny planes
of the prince albert bomber training school
training to deal out death to defend against it

we were part of a larger world of horror
how could i ten years old
understand there were men who would
never come back?

in the abandoned rcmp barracks soldiers
in army uniform lived and marched
down our streets zombies we called them
because they would not fight foreign wars
they would fight only to defend our own
canadian borders they were
forced to march the streets in shame and
children were encouraged to taunt them
with names like coward
i stared because they were all from
somewhere so far away they were from new
brunswick quebec and prince edward
island misery written
on their ordinary faces

having reached three score and ten
near the last page of my book
i wake up to the full impact of this world
where war is never over

mass murder in yugoslavia in east timor
in africa killing in ireland in palestine and
the children killing children

we've landed on the moon we've got e-mails
you and i can readily fly to hong kong
or new york the world has changed
it's so much smaller than it was
when i was ten

this tiny planet looks so peaceful
so beautiful from outer space

but who can say hurray
when our old enemy is
still the human heart?

i wake up
to the sadness
of being seventy.

The Red Buddha

IV

THE WILD WEST
OF THE NORTH

american continent is full
of rock caves--desperadoes,
living legends lived in--
hiding out from the law,
the armies. living in the canyons
in dark holes and hollows
squinting at the horizon
for a row of armed men

the c.i.a. today
the f.b.i.
the desperadoes aren't hiding
in the old holes and canyons
they have secret street addresses
and secret telephone numbers
you could pass one on the street
without knowing
you could brush by one
at the supermarket without knowing
you could even look in the mirror
without knowing

until
they
break
down
your
door

AUGUST
AFTERNOON

They are sitting in their coffins
On the balcony
Chatting amiably
And graciously the way
Superior persons do
And they continue the conversation
Now that the coffins are closed
And while Madame Recamier
Is sitting up in her coffin
On her chaise lounge
Talking about Napoleon while
Her feet do not reach the
Footstool anymore
She is nailed inside the box of
Her nostalgia while a man
In a good dark suit and dark
Wings leans over the railing
Of Waterloo Bridge while
Behind him a lion which
May or may not be alive sits on the
Sidewalk like a cat looking
At us

It is done by magnification
And luminosity
And mirrors do have something to do
With it and ashes volcanic ashes

A huge boulder floats through the air
The waves wash under it
The clouds move behind it
High up on top of it there
Is a medieval castle
It is not possible
Two monsters have emerged from the sea
And they are singing a song of love
The boulder is moving to the Alps
Where we think it will feel
More at home
Spring is moving in a dress of flowers
Walking in barefeet
And it is raining men in Homburgs
A woman on horseback
Is riding through the woods
Which are opening like
Venetian blinds
Vertically
Memory is a spider walking
Up the side of a statue

CERILLOS

on hot adobe walls
a dozen lizards dozing vertically

wind sculpted sands turquoise country

a parrot whose name is kermit
recites his name over and over
or hello hello hello

nighty the black cat keeps away from him
so does the three-legged dog
and the hawk who drops down
from the sky gently on ron's head

after a year of feeding
and healing him
ron let him go

up into the atmosphere
where he disappeared
but he still comes down

out of nowhere
when ron whistles

DIVINING TRAY

friend from nigeria
ignores or never gives a thought
to that don't touch rule
here at the exhibition
of african art
he walks up to the divining tray
and talks about it
as though he's at home
and this is his

security guard blackman
wearing blue
indignant (somewhat)
rushes up
hears the yoruba in the english sounds
something makes him
feel
respect
for this black african man
holding up the carved
divining tray

he tells me how the
future is told on it

his father took him
many times to have his future told
with just such a tray as this

i listen so does
security guard

THAT'S NOT BURT LANCASTER UP THERE

You said and our teeth glittered
In our laughter. You gouged out this
Black and white woodcut Jesus
And I told you it was a cliché
And that nobody could do anything
With it anymore and besides
Your Jesus looks like
A hunk of meat, like
Rembrandt's bloody ox
And I don't want to look at it
And you said "Good That's
What I want" and I told you
Over and over how repulsive
It was and you said "Good"
And you said it over
And over
While Christ's head fell
Into the basket of his ribs
Encircled with a crown of
Stabbing thorns
Above his castrated humanity
And you made me see
It wasn't Burt Lancaster
Or anything meek and mild

AT THE GROCERY CHECKOUT COUNTER

standing next to my items
waiting my turn to pay
i am offended
we have not come a long way baby

baby nothing much has changed
women's magazines continue to put
good and gooey dark chocolate cake on the cover
right next to the promise you can lose ten pounds
in time for bathing suit weather with the added
promise to reveal bedroom secrets to please
your man and how to prepare the perfect
lattice top blueberry pie how to inflame
his desire with the right perfume the right
bustier how to tempt him luscious desserts
it's still so much all about him

those same old formulas those same old
crazy making mixed messages
those cheap fantasies become a beach beauty

in five weeks those same pictures
of ultra slim women in ultra expensive
dresses
that fuck you look on their faces

they know they've got us every which way
they know we'll buy they know we'll pay
they know they'll profit

it is so depressing
exiting safeway i scoop it up
my tiny handful of change

WHEN I SAID THE BEVERLY HILLS BUTLER

was playing the role of a butler
the psychologist didn't understand
no, i didn't mean a film performance
i meant letting me in the door
the butler was playing the role of a butler
that simple
and after i talked to him some more
he stopped playing the role of the butler
the psychologist frowned at that
and i told him
right now you are playing the role
of a psychologist and his frowns
dug deeper into his forehead
and i, i said, i am playing the role
of a sick housewife, right?
and i laughed
but he didn't laugh
i laughed loud enough
for both of us
he stared at me
i laughed my belly bursting
cosmic laugh
including both of us in the joke

hearing my laughter from the other
side of the wall i imagine
my laughter makes his flesh creep a little
as he adjusts his coat and tie
he knows i'm insane
because i could be out and free
if only i took him seriously
after all
he is in charge
of reality
(he has the key)

he shudders walking away from me
(but it's all part of his profession)
he shrugs and adjusts his coat

I MENTIONED INDIANS

and
he instantly jumped into
his freud formula suit with usc decorations
wild irrational forces of the id
and the unconscious
the way
he immediately put it
one word
had pushed his id button

but i don't
come from detroit
like he does

when i walked down the streets of
prince albert
saskatchewan
and saw a dark fat soft woman
wearing purple and long braids
walking in moccasins
on cement
i didn't see a
dark force of the id of the
unconscious stalking the grey
sidewalk past harradence's hardware and
the central fruit and candy kitchen

i saw a dark soft woman walking

sometimes i said tonsaygwa
and she said midorsin migeesegau

maybe
his freud formula is valid
maybe it's valid

but only with reservations

AMONG
THE GREAT
HEADS

on pedestals in the egyptian gallery
they were carved from rock black
and smooth as obsidian white as alabaster
and all the granite greys between

we sat among them as they gazed upon us
through the distance of time
we breathed in their silence of centuries

there the poet carolyn kizer read to us
conjuring up two girls in the dazzle
of young womanhood
two girls in love with the sun with the brisk wind
so far from home
carrying exotic intoxicating scents
two girls with long sunbrowned legs
in love with themselves and who they would be
in love with the aegean sailors and the sea

life opening itself up to them
and they opening themselves

i look at the fringed hem of her skirt and
smile
i look at her and smile at the wild girl she
was
at the wise woman she is

the egyptians have heard it all before
they smile at the surprise the freshness of it

they are always waiting
to hear this again

MEETING
FOR THE
FIRST TIME

the zen master
high in the hierarchy
of vietnamese buddhism
bowed briefly in his brown robes
i inclined my head in return

we walked into his garden
and he laughed again a chunk
of that
enormous laugh we laughed together
until i realized only
the two of us
were laughing in
the roomful of people
and i suddenly stopped
and so did he
and we
merely smiled

now walking in the garden
laughing he waves his hand
toward the red blades of gladioli
over the green grass

this he says is a fine place
for buddha to meditate

don't you think he asks
that this is a fine place for
buddha to meditate?

THE PART OF
HER THAT IS
SILENT

is speaking
she does not know it is her voice
a cooing from the ceiling
a marimba that can barely be heard
sounding through the floor
from downstairs

the silent part of her
learning to speak
frightens her
the cooing will not stop
the marimba will not stop

she must listen to
the silent part of her

she must listen to
the sounds of her
not yet words
that insist

this voice
she does not know
is hers

YOU ARE
FRIGHTENED
OF MY WILD
TEARS

you tell me that what it is
you don't like about me
is the way i get angry so unexpectedly
and so savagely
you tell me i am like the girl
with the curl
in the middle of her forehead
when she is good she is very very good
and when she is bad she is horrid
whatever i am i am never between
it is always this or that
and you can't stand that
lack of moderation
(i don't ask my wild tears to justify me
and i don't call you back
i ride with the sun and the moon
with shadowless noon
and the space of midnight
and all those unnoticed
hours between when i am merely
peeling onions washing dishes

making a bed setting a table
or cleaning the floor)
WHAT YOU CAN'T UNDERSTAND
is why i no longer look up at you
that's what leaves you perplexed
and feeling unfamiliar (in your own house)
you were always comfortable enough
(with my tears)
(with my tantrums)

THE LUST
FOR MURDER

and the undecided question
why didn't i do it

sometimes wisely thinking
good thing i didn't
and yet

and yet sometimes i admit
the clean finality of murder
appeals to my aesthetic
sensibility the very thought
of it satisfies my soul
the way legal
arrangements do not

times i want a knife
in my hand
a stone dagger
and i will be a priestess
and he will lie on the operating
table and i will bring
my hand down from where
it was fully raised in the air
and i will make an incision
in his chest
and with my hand
remove his red beating heart
and raise it up while

the blood flows down
my arm over my white robes

and then
i will feed it to
the lowest of the animals

that's what i wanted
not what happened in
the courtroom where i signed
my name to the pages
of papers and it was all
over and my left hand had to
hold the right hand by the wrist
so it would be steady
enough to sign

oh no it was not a pen
i wanted in my hand

STILL LIFE
WITH ELVIS

watching that fifties flick
the plot so thin it's laughable
but who cares?
the whole point is watching elvis
every move he makes his body speaks
a new language the old folks can't take the voltage
of his charm aimed right at us

ed sullivan blocked those legs that twisting torso
in the living rooms of america
even half of him is too much
right here and now elvis promises
we are the declaration of independence
why wouldn't we go wild with it?

a dime in the juke box for all shook up
my son four years old gets the beat bouncing
and bobbing so into it the other coffee shop
patrons perched on their stools
cracking up totally

later larry and glenda telling me we saw elvis
and his wife
at the self-realization temple in pacific palisades
it was there my son now the accomplished
photographer took photos of swans charging
across the water in a storm of feathers

years later i'm divorced working with linda

in the legal office in san francisco
the two of us head for lake tahoe
the cocktail waiter puts three glasses
of tequila sunrise on the table for linda
three gin and tonics for me the lights dim
there he is in the spotlight doing
his hawaiian stuff dazzling in that white suit
i am living on the river of his voice
he's still got it that electric charge

throwing scarves wet with elvis sweat
into the audience
when we leave linda whispers if only
she'd given the usher a twenty just maybe
we could've had a front row seat and gotten one
of those scarves she asks a woman who did get one
would you sell it?
that woman smiles in total triumph
no way

1977 up there in northern saskatchewan
a man drags his canoe across the gravel road
from a lake on one side to the lake on the other side
he disappears across impossibly glossy water
gary turns the radio on
we hear it
elvis is dead

years later gary tells me you're the one
i was with when elvis died

2002 i'm watching that fifties elvis flick
loving every living minute of him

MARILYN!
I WAS DRIVING
SCARED

through the mohave my rear view
mirror said divorce i couldn't see
anything ahead but trouble i couldn't
see anything but i drove
on through
between the broken

twisted limbs of joshua trees and
red tipped ocotillo tumbleweed rolling
over the road spiny cactus pushing up
the radio crackled

telling me your death

where sand shimmers and waves
and bends and everything is
a heat mirage there where

night is knife cold
the radio telling
me your death

marilyn! you walk
in high heeled shoes
that fill with sand

and you stand
on one leg
remove a shoe and let the
sand spill out laughing and
then you do
the other shoe

marilyn! your smile

gets larger your laugh
gets more powerful you
get stronger
your blonde body wiggling

as though the statue of liberty
has finally come

to some kind of life

engraved luminous
in our hearts

THE GOOD LITTLE GINGERBREAD GIRLS

and boys
of my childhood
are gone
the little white houses we lived in
are gone
the trees are gone

when i was back there
10 years ago
staying 40 miles north of there

with friends from
all over canada and the united states
(we believed we were painters
then and some of us were

one of us had three one man shows going
one in brussels another one in london
and a third in new york
we were up there
in the muskeg and pinewoods
the lake and midnight halos
of northern lights weaving
through thick stars)

so while
i was in the safeway store
in that little hometown
40 miles south, my arms
full of giant soda bottles
someone rushed up
and addressed me by name
to my surprise

i looked at him
and no i couldn't
remember him

stuart mackey he was
stuart mackey
i remember the name

how he sat two desks
away when we were kids
at queen mary school
yes
well, now he's the manager

of this safeway
i look around at it
as though it isn't quite
like every other safeway
this is stuart mackey's safeway

and then he tells me
bubbling with excitement
phyllis putsey married gordon goodall
orlean o'leary married ...
everybody married somebody else
he tells me where each
couple lives
harry tatlow and gladys
live on the hill on 20th street
and it goes on and on
amazing, i am amazed

i am so amazed
my arms start to open slightly
in amazement
and two quart bottles of coca-cola
crash to the floor

and there is glass
and foam and brown
liquid all over his floor
beside the frozen foods
and i apologize my god
what have i done
but no, no, it's okay

he says, it's okay
and he dashes for the mop
and dashes back

i stand there
listening
while he mops and talks

and as i walk over
to the cash register
he's still sweeping up
bits of broken glass

i drive northward
toward the surreal
silence of the lake

IF YOU READ HANS CHRISTIAN ANDERSEN

there's this little gerda
in the story called the snow queen
and she takes off and travels
all over the map
doesn't stay locked up in a tower
at all
instead she travels everywhere
just by herself
and meets very strange people
who are all one way or another
helpful to her
and they all want her to stay
but she insists
on moving on

you see she's trying to find
her good friend little kai
and finally she does
there he is at the north pole
trying to solve the immense
ice puzzle of reason
(ever since that sliver of glass
became embedded in his heart)

she finally found him
threw her arms around him
and her warm tears melted
the sliver in his heart

and suddenly somehow
the whole ice puzzle fell into place
and he was free
and they were both happy
and together went back
to a warmer place.

***

all the men i know
have slivers in their hearts
but my tears do not have those magical effects

the only men i know
whose hearts are healthy
are african
and the way things turn out
we wind up
with continents or oceans between us
remembering each other very well
and that's something

and much better than being married
to a scientist for 15 years
who still takes pride in
that glass sliver in his heart
working painstakingly in his laboratory
long after midnight
trying to pry open
further secrets of the atomic nucleus

***

my tears are without magic
my arms not warm enough

EVEN WHEN
HE TOLD ME
ABOUT HIS
OPERA CAPE

I didn't believe him
Even when I saw the way his teeth grew
I didn't believe it
Even when he smashed my front door
And stood in broken glass
Staring at me
His eyes glowing dark coals of
Evil
I thought it was an act
I didn't take it seriously
An idiosyncrasy I thought
He just couldn't scare me
I thought it was all operatic
My neighbor said he's mentally unbalanced
And i asked how can you tell?
Just by looking at him he said
And I laughed again

Finally one day in the surf
Off San Pedro I too saw it
Finally
I was standing against the rocks
Thigh deep in water
And he was standing higher

Maybe 8 feet away
We were talking laughing looking at each
other
And suddenly
I turned and looked
And an immense claw
Of a wave was
Coming down
White heavy huge violence
And no way
For me to get out
Of the way
And I clung to
The rock I looked
Into his eyes
He didn't move
His eyelids didn't flicker
His eyes were cool and curious
And as that wave
Smashed down
On me
I knew him
The water ripped against me
And the rough rock
Ripped against me
I bent and crumpled but
I held my footing
The wave water pounding
Boiling against me
And then the wave
Moved back

Swirling slowly
Round my thighs again
And I looked into his
Eyes
Walked toward him
Still swaying with shock
He had not even
Cried out to warn me
My body was bleeding
But I was alive
There was nothing I could do
He said
Nothing I could do
I couldn't get to you
He said
I didn't say you didn't try
I saw his eyes
Lizard eyes vampire eyes
Dead eyes
Behind the silly
swirls
Of his opera cape
Dead eyes

THE ATOM BOMB FINALLY WENT OFF

in my brain
it took long enough to detonate

with all my senses i suddenly realized
that the inside
of my living skull
is political territory
that the landscape of my brain
whatever else it is
is a colony of corporate america

when it all happened
when i suddenly finally
saw
it wasn't like

comes the dawn

no gentle light

but the desert blazing with brightness
that blinding flash of
actual insight
that blew my synapses
and made me see

just what kind of conquered
territory i am
and who has stuck their flag
into my side

Alamogordo

a thousand thousand suns

all the mornings of my life

compressed into one

the horizon a line of fire

get a geiger counter
and measure me

my brainwaves have been altered
i am radioactive
and glow in the dark
photograph my bones
see me a bright skeleton
moving against the dark
white as light

BRIDGE ACROSS

the mississippi
route 66 through st louis
stainless steel arch glinting
behind us as we cross over
totally freaked out on
acid grass each other and the whole
cosmos like we were holding
handfuls of the cosmos in
our hands and we knew it
that we were as real as
the clouds magnificently over
st louis and the water was full of
boats steamboats rowboats
ferryboats canoes sailboats
every kind of boat and
even huck finn's raft
we had breakfast in carthage
missouri
the guy at the gas station
a few miles back had looked
at us very
funny and went in to get our change
and when he didn't come
back out i went in to see
what was happening and he
was talking on the phone and
in carthage where we had
breakfast suddenly five cops
came in and i wasn't

even worried about the several
hundred caps of acid or the
grass because god was
with us all the way
and there were lines around
us no cop could cross
we looked at them
and then i told you about
the roses growing
in my garden in california and you
told me about your garden in the
commune
on mount washington and we
laughed at the blue plastic
bachelor buttons planted
beside our booth but the
breakfast was good and
the cops left and we each
had a second cup of
hot chocolate before we
continued on our way

WE WERE
TWINS
IN THE

womb of the same mother
we were that close
no, closer he said
closer than twins in the same
womb i have often thought
he said how we are closer
than that and we know
we share one soul
we were not even conscious of
being close we were that close
that our breaths intermingled
is irrelevant
the monuments of old arguments
crumbled
that shaky record
and how the hand of time
but those who know, know
there is no bridge back
to ignorance there is no bridge
back to that shore

to go back
would be to imagine bridges
to imagine some security
and those imaginings that
way *does* madness lie

and foul and withering death

no dancer, i did that dance
for him
i showed him all seven
veils
so that he could learn
to see through them
i appeared to him
as a white crane
and reflected in water
and he gasped at the
first sight of it
and smiled with my smile

i showed him myself
in my black long dress
with the hundreds
of tiny buttons
i was afraid they would
be too much for him
but he unbuttoned them one
by one from my
throat down
to my ankles
seeing my nakedness

i put on his grey vest
over my breasts
and his brown felt hat
on my head

and we sat by the fireplace
watching the flames
while your lips and fingers
like a delicious sacrilege
lingered over the landscape
of my body and you
studied the pools of my eyes
looking for secrets
looking for love

i put on her silks
flowered with jungles
and the wild animals
and their beauty
and the awesomeness
of that journey
was between us
clear and beautiful
as a map drawn
with hands shimmering

and then that dress
like poured cream so
smooth and soft
with the winedark
fastenings
this you said
your hands smooth
over the smoothness
covering me with its
sweet glistening this you said

as though from the banquet
of the cosmos on which
we were feasting you would
if you had to
choose only one you would
choose this this you said
is my favorite
we could have stayed there
while the match flame burned
how far did we go together?
even the astronomers
do not have those numbers
we have them here
before the match burns down

every hour, he said, everything
changes completely
he was beginning
to understand
he was beginning
to see
it was the thinnest veil

then we walked
through the door together
and sat down
looking up into the sky
around us
and the clouds danced
and moved and formed
and reformed before
our eyes with all the

colors of sunset moving
towards us so close

we were closer than twins
in the womb
of the same mother
closer than twins
in the womb of the
infinite void

and there was no fear
in his eyes

i cannot tell you
what there was in his eyes

LONG WAY BACK

all the way to the short legs
of the toddler the tired toddler
i refuse to walk any further
an act of refusal i will walk
no further

my mother pops the pyramidal orange
and green crocheted tea cosy on my head
now be a good soldier
march she says
but i will not be a soldier
i will not march i refuse

my mother carrying the sack of groceries
puts it down
there beside that wrought iron fence
and picks up my baby sister in her arms

i climb up into the stroller
and that
is my first memory

and i remember how when
we got there where my father
was building our house
there was a fire
and the frying pan with liver
and onions in it

and there was the sun
and the sky

and everything

DEATH IS ALWAYS THE LAST SURPRISE

my father they tell me was sprawled
on the bathroom floor when the ambulance
arrived my mother told them
he's been through enough already
don't bring him back

but she didn't want him taken away
she waited until the next day to call
the funeral people
his body strapped in a vertical position
my mother marveled how he went
out of his house on his feet
in a rig with little wheels

fire consumed his flesh
what was left that you could touch
tiny bone splinters crumbs of ash
compacted in the smallest box

that day the tide was out at rathtrevor beach
a thin skin of shining water over the sand
where i walked it went out and out
then suddenly dropped off down deep
another place altogether steep and dark

i paused at the edge looking across bright
water
into infinite sky and then i turned
to walk back to shore back to
the forest of dark trees

that day even the sun told me
he's no longer here

that day
my father was everywhere

ROCKED

rocked nine months
in the soft cradle of
my mother's body
become big with the
mystery of me
rocked nine months toward my
birthcry

nine months more whirled in this world and there
i am
in the old photo
walking on my own two feet
so happy to be
walking in this world
that expression of pure
is it self-congratulation
that i was to see
on my son's face
when he
mastered the art of
locomotion crawling
full speed across
the whole floor
happiness in each
slap of the hand down
as he
moved forward
that glorious glee
in his laugh

god! he was going!

so there i am
nine months old
a walking talking kid
those little shoes
and socks my mother bending down
holding one hand
a big flower
in my other
small paw

looking at that photo
i can see the whole cosmos
sparkle around me
glowing out like the heart
of the flower
gold as the sun
in my fist

my mother's sweet
and gentle smile
high above me
shining down

GRAND CANYON

its rainbows make
postcards to fly home

its vastness crows fly

the ranger explains the equation
between altitude and latitude

he tantalizes with stories of the north
so much higher
so high everything on the kaibab plateau
has flora and fauna of the canadian
rockies plus a squirrel found nowhere
else this squirrel black
and white is sometimes mistaken for a skunk

birch trees spruce quaking
aspens populate the density of forests
not piñon pine

my son and i absorb lessons
around the flames of the fire
and he begins to put on the pressure
he wants to get to the other side
of the grand canyon he wants us
to ride burros down to the bottom
along a thin trail of next to nothing
on one side

under the burros' feet gravel
slips sideways and all the way
down the fact is my son is only ten
and needs to be eleven to legally
go on this trip he wants to talk
me into lying about his age he
knows i've done it before this
time it's his idea i tell him the
reason for this rule is insurance

the insurance won't cover
if something happens and they find
out we lied but he's willing
to take his chances he doesn't care about
insurance he knows i hate insurance
companies myself he knows i have total
contempt for them and their tall buildings
they put up in downtown los angeles
the truth is i'm glad he's only ten
not eleven when i wouldn't have
a chance when i would have to get
my ass on a burro pointing straight
down it isn't so much
healthy fear and a wish to preserve my life

it is that i know beyond
the slightest doubt the part of my anatomy
most directly involved with the burro
wouldn't be able to tolerate four or
more hours on the back of a moving
beast of no great intelligence knowing
that beast would probably not of its own free

will have chosen to do this either the
burro would be coerced under
duress i know my rear is not in shape
for it i know it would be in
agony of sore aching screaming muscles in
ten minutes' time and i wouldn't be able
to get out of the saddle
it is a formula for torture

i tell my son no i can't lie about
your age not today try it he says try
it he's telling me he'll respect
me more as a mother if i just try to lie
on his behalf and i understand what
he's saying i understand how much

he wants to go down that narrow
path twisting down for literally miles
how he doesn't give a thought
to what his own bottom will feel like
he doesn't have to he knows his happiness
will more than compensate for any
physical discomfort if he even stops
to think about that aspect of what
he is proposing

his arguments fizzle down to nothing
because it is not his age that is
the crucial concern it is the aspect
of my anatomy that knows its
limits that has not been designed

for this and doesn't want
to be initiated into burro
riding beginning with a monumental
trip hairpins straight down for two
terrifying miles no i won't go no we
won't go and that is that but he
keeps at me watching the lucky ones
get on their animals looking at me
accusingly i know i have the
insurance company and all the regulations
on my side i have everything i've
always despised and flouted whenever
i could and he knows it my
integrity takes the long fall

i am not going to tell him it's my
anatomy the fact is also i would
probably get on a burro whose name
is jennie and she would somehow
put her left foot down in
such a way that she would for a
moment lose her balance and fail
to regain it and we would descend
together off the trail rapidly
disappearing and the buzzards would
begin to circle the mist would rise
and a rainbow would become our
epitaph

i don't want my son to lose his mother
that way

forget it i tell him i'm not getting on
a burro

we go into the bright angel lodge and
order trout with green beans mixed
with toasted slivers of almonds
everything is beautiful and tastes great
he glares at me in a friendly manner
he knows he is defeated he simply
doesn't have the arsenal of arguments
to deal with my stubbornness i know
he is thinking about what it will
be like to be eleven to qualify
legally he's thinking what it will
be like to be grownup to be an
adult to be free to make his own
decisions to be able to deal with the
grand canyon on his own terms
he sees himself on that burro
going downhill through spectacular scenery

that night after the ranger talks about
the north side of the canyon again
he urges me we really should go there
it's obviously the most interesting side
and fewer people go there and
it is like canada and can we go?

i take out our maps and
i show him look i say
crow flying it's twelve miles
straight across but for us it's two

hundred miles do you realize that?
it's a two hundred mile drive through the
desert we have to loop around this
way he smiles at me he knows i can't
say no this time he smiles his smile
of sweet victory

the next day
we are driving by dome-shaped dirt-colored
hogans in the desert
we are driving through the kaibab
plateau of utah and it does look
like canada

WASN'T ONLY MY MOTHER GAVE BIRTH TO ME

but i was closer
to my father's rib bone
than any part of her
and he gave birth to
part of me
she would rather not see

you're just like your father
she'd say the cutting edge
of anger in her voice
you're not like me she'd say
you're some throwback from way back
she'd say like i was
a creature from the blue lagoon
or somewhere not out of her womb

and she was right
i felt the blue air of the sky
part of my bones, felt
the rivers in my blood
felt the sun pouring into my pores

it wasn't only my mother
gave birth to me
even that husband

164 MAIA PENFOLD/The Red Buddha

brought part of me into being
that had never
been there before
and holding my infant son in my arms
wasn't i born with his birth
into being a mother
and the whole cosmos was a new place
born with his birth

many births in one lifetime
many deaths and the flow between
birth and death
flow between death and birth
until the final immunity
when the cosmos opens
once and for all
and we're here for the first time
fully ourselves
miles beyond the rivers the mountains
miles beyond the last words

DOING THE DANCE

death touching and teasing
getting close
final power of the unknown hour

little by little the litany of losses
more and more everything goes
eyes weaken
ears fail teeth disappear
even bones give out
hip replaced

yet what's strange and quirky
my hair still not grey
i can't figure that one out

pushing 75 pulling 74
i'm here reading obituaries

i've got those long lived genes

in the year 1900 there she is
rock of gibraltar great great grandmother
photographed at 98
(when the average female lifespan
was less than half of that)

my own mother's now 96
her sister my aunt anna
lived to 98

i've got those long lived genes
(i'm beating the odds so far)
death's got a long ways to go
with me

death's got a long dance
to do

INSTRUCTIONS TO MY SON

The day will come
Not for an expensive box
Dropped into a hole in the ground
Covered up with dirt

My choice is cremation
Fire and flame
Down to clean ash
Sharp bits of bone

In Colorado or Oregon
Climb a convenient mountain
To a seaward rushing stream
Put me in its mountain music
And let me go

To join with everything

Everywhere